Luck of the Draw

A Play

A. S. Robertson

A Samuel French Acting Edition

SAMUELFRENCH.COM
SAMUELFRENCH-LONDON.CO.UK

Copyright © 2007 by A. S. Robertson
All Rights Reserved

LUCK OF THE DRAW is fully protected under the copyright laws of the United States of America, the British Commonwealth, including Canada, and all other countries of the Copyright Union. All rights, including professional and amateur stage productions, recitation, lecturing, public reading, motion picture, radio broadcasting, television and the rights of translation into foreign languages are strictly reserved.

ISBN 978-0-573-02379-8

www.SamuelFrench.com
www.SamuelFrench-London.co.uk

FOR PRODUCTION ENQUIRIES

UNITED STATES AND CANADA
Info@SamuelFrench.com
1-866-598-8449

UNITED KINGDOM AND EUROPE
Theatre@SamuelFrench-London.co.uk
020-7255-4302

Each title is subject to availability from Samuel French, depending upon country of performance. Please be aware that *LUCK OF THE DRAW* may not be licensed by Samuel French in your territory. Professional and amateur producers should contact the nearest Samuel French office or licensing partner to verify availability.

CAUTION: Professional and amateur producers are hereby warned that *LUCK OF THE DRAW* is subject to a licensing fee. Publication of this play does not imply availability for performance. Both amateurs and professionals considering a production are strongly advised to apply to Samuel French before starting rehearsals, advertising, or booking a theatre. A licensing fee must be paid whether the titleis presented for charity or gain and whether or not admission is charged. Professional/Stock licensing fees are quoted upon application to Samuel French.

No one shall make any changes in this title for the purpose of production. No part of this book may be reproduced, stored in a retrieval system, or transmitted in any form, by any means, now known or yet to be invented, including mechanical, electronic, photocopying, recording, videotaping, or otherwise, without the prior written permission of the publisher. No one shall upload this title, or part of this title, to any social media websites.

For all enquiries regarding motion picture, television, and other media rights, please contact Samuel French.

MUSIC USE NOTE

Licensees are solely responsible for obtaining formal written permission from copyright owners to use copyrighted music in the performance of this play and are strongly cautioned to do so. If no such permission is obtained by the licensee, then the licensee must use only original music that the licensee owns and controls. Licensees are solely responsible and liable for all music clearances and shall indemnify the copyright owners of the play and their licensing agent, Samuel French, against any costs, expenses, losses and liabilities arising from the use of music by licensees. Please contact the appropriate music licensing authority in your territory for the rights to any incidental music.

IMPORTANT BILLING AND CREDIT REQUIREMENTS

If you have obtained performance rights to this title, please refer to your licensing agreement for important billing and credit requirements.

CHARACTERS

Wilf, chairman of the committee
Ronnie, treasurer
Mrs Bannion, organizer
Mr Pessel, visiting member

The action of the play takes place in the committee room of the Shelf Union Social Club.

Time—the present, approaching Christmas

LUCK OF THE DRAW

The committee room. Approaching Christmas

In the centre of the room is a long table with four hard chairs. On the opposite side of the entrance door is a smaller table upon which are the prizes for the raffle. First prize is a large food hamper with a bottle of whisky and a bottle of sherry. Various bottles and boxes of chocolates make up the other prizes

The sound of voices approaching the room is heard. A key goes into the lock and the door opens

Pause

Wilf (*off*) Would you like to go in first, Mr Pessel?
Mr Pessel (*off*) OK.

Mr Pessel enters. He walks slowly into the room and stops to look around

Wilf (*off*) You're satisfied you're the only person in the room, Mr Pessel?
Mr Pessel Yes. Oh yes, no doubt about that.

Wilf enters. He turns to the open door

You can come in now, Ronnie!

Ronnie enters carrying a large tin box with a padlock, containing raffle tickets, which he places on the large table

Wilf You can lock the door now, Mr Pessel.
Ronnie Best wait for Mrs Bannion.
Wilf Where is she?

Mr Pessel wanders over to the prize table

Mr Pessel These are your prizes then?
Wilf We won't go to that table until secretary's present
Mr Pessel Good quality of prize though. Even the smaller ones be worth having.
Wilf (*to Ronnie*) Gone to the toilet has she?
Ronnie Could have gone earlier.
Wilf Deliberate isn't it? Wants to be noticed. She can't come into a room without making an entrance.
Ronnie Time enough to inform Mr Pessel — of conditions.
Wilf (*turning formally to Mr Pessel*) You understand, Mr Pessel why you've been invited here tonight?
Mr Pessel Oh yes.
Wilf To make the draw on our Christmas raffle, yes, but also to act as an independent witness to the fairness of the proceedings. In your role as non-committee member of this club, it will be your duty to speak out against anything you consider to be unfair or dishonest. You understand that?
Mr Pessel I do.
Wilf And you're quite satisfied with the proceedings so far?
Mr Pessel Oh yes, more than satisfied. To be honest, I'd no idea you went to this trouble.
Ronnie Good cause for it, Mr Pessel. Always a few among those who don't win — try to spread rumours — fictions to undermine our integrity.
Mr Pessel Well, I see it's all above board so far.
Wilf That's how we intend to keep it and why Ronnie hasn't taken his eye off that ticket box since he brought it from the safe. We have a ——

Mrs Bannion enters loudly and looking flushed

Mrs Bannion Sorry! Didn't know you had gone in! I was organizing the notice-board. Didn't hear any of you shout for me!
Wilf Lock the door now, Mr Pessel.

Mrs Bannion goes straight to the prize table

Mrs Bannion Somebody been touching these prizes? That shouldn't be there.

While Mrs Bannion fusses about with the prizes, Mr Pessel is locking the door

Wilf Before you do, Mr Pessel, I should say, this may take some time. If anyone else has the urge to — organize the notice-board they should do it now, or keep it for later.

Pause

Right, lock up!

Mr Pessel locks up

Mr Pessel (*taken with the seriousness of the proceedings*) Now will I leave the key in the lock, or would you like it brought to the table?
Wilf In the door will be fine.
Mr Pessel That's it then. All locked up.
Wilf If we all take our seats. (*Indicating*) You sit there, Mr Pessel.

The three men sit while Mrs Bannion remains at the prize table

Are you with us, Mrs Bannion?
Mrs Bannion I've got a better idea for arranging these tins. Building up at the back looks nice but you see what's going to happen as soon as the hamper is lifted — some of these grapes are bruised already.
Mr Pessel You chose the hamper, Mrs Bannion?
Mrs Bannion Oh yes. I select all the food.

Mr Pessel It's quality food. I can see that.
Mrs Bannion Not as good as I would have liked. They make you work to a budget, see. Some of them don't know what food costs.
Mr Pessel I'll bet you do.

Wilf hands a sheet of paper to Mr Pessel

Wilf Sign your name and status, Mr Pessel.
Mr Pessel My what?
Wilf Member — put member across from your signature.
Ronnie That way we have evidence of everybody in attendance — in case of any recriminations. Anyone with a complaint would be able to go to anyone on the list.
Wilf This will be on the notice-board tomorrow with the list of prize winners.
Mr Pessel It's a responsibility, isn't it?
Ronnie Ever drawn a raffle before?
Mr Pessel I can't say I have.
Ronnie Best that way.

Mrs Bannion returns to her seat

Mrs Bannion I'm not entirely happy with the selection. But I don't think anyone could have done better on the budget. We'll have to allow more for tinned foods next year, Wilf. I can't always have the time to hunt down the best offers.
Wilf We'll make a note of that, Mrs Bannion. Now ...
Mrs Bannion (*to Mr Pessel*) You can get bashed tins cheaper but you can't put them in a prize — you couldn't.

Pause

Wilf If we're ready, I'll begin. We're here tonight on behalf of the Shelf Union Social Club to make the draw for the Christmas raffle. I'd like to extend a welcome to our scrutinizing member Mr Pessel.
Mrs Bannion Hear hear.

Luck of the Draw

Wilf What we will ask you to do, Mr Pessel, is draw five tickets from that box. The first ticket you draw will be for the first prize, the food hamper and two bottles of whisky.
Mrs Bannion No — bottle of whisky and bottle of sherry.
Wilf Since when?
Ronnie It's on the tickets, Wilf.
Wilf Any reason for that?
Mrs Bannion More women in the club.
Wilf That's all to the good.
Mrs Bannion Some of them complained last year.
Mr Pessel I can understand that.
Mrs Bannion Got to attract the women.
Mr Pessel I find vodka does that.
Wilf Anyway, that's the first prize — the second ticket for the second prize and so on ... Is that clear?
Mr Pessel Yes.
Wilf Test the padlock!
Mr Pessel Test?
Wilf Pull on it, man.

Pessel tugs at the padlock on the box

Got the key, Ronnie?

Ronnie produces a brown envelope from his inside pocket. Wilf takes the envelope and holds it towards Mr Pessel

Inside this sealed envelope is the key, Mr Pessel. This envelope was placed in the safe before the first ticket was put in that box.

Wilf places the envelope slowly on top of the box and then there is a pause. They all stare at the envelope

Open the box, Mr Pessel.

Mr Pessel very slowly tears open the envelope. He retrieves the key, inserts it in the padlock on the box and opens the padlock

Now open the box.

Mrs Bannion Shouldn't we shake it first? I understood we always shook the box.
Ronnie I don't think so.
Mrs Bannion Did last year.
Wilf No, we talked about shaking it last year, but as I pointed out, by the time it was carried upstairs — it already had a good shaking.
Mrs Bannion Not the way Ronnie carried it up it didn't. I watched you — you were very careful not to shake it.
Ronnie I was careful, yes, but I think more from fear of dropping the box, than upsetting the tickets inside.
Wilf Is this really important?
Mrs Bannion Fair's fair.
Wilf If you consider ——
Mrs Bannion I'm thinking of the last person to buy a ticket. That'll be the one on top.
Ronnie I wouldn't think so.
Wilf And anyway, Mr Pessel isn't necessarily going to pick the top one. Are you, Mr Pessel?
Mr Pessel I hadn't worked out a plan ...
Mrs Bannion You might have though.
Mr Pessel Well eh ...
Ronnie I don't think it's in order for us to tell him how to pick a ticket.
Mrs Bannion What do you normally do?
Ronnie He's never done it before.
Wilf If we're going to be in dispute about this, the fairest thing would be to let the man himself decide. What do you think, Mr Pessel: do you think the box should be shaken or left as it is now — which is not to say it's unshaken now — but do you think it should be shaken further?

Pause

Mr Pessel Well — I suppose a little shaking wouldn't do it any harm — then again as you say, Mr Chairman, it's probably been shaken quite a bit already — I'm not fussy either way.
Ronnie It's not for your benefit we're asking, Mr Pessel.

Luck of the Draw   7

Mr Pessel Oh no.
Ronnie The committee is undecided. That's why we're asking you.
Mr Pessel Of course.

Pause

Ronnie Well?
Mr Pessel If I'm pushed for a decision — I'd be inclined towards giving it a shake — a little shake.
Wilf Give it a shake then.
Mr Pessel Me?

Mr Pessel, under the gaze of the others, gives the box a quick shake

Wilf Is that it?
Mr Pessel Just a — little shake.
Wilf Hardly worth bothering about, was it?
Mrs Bannion I thought you would have given it more of a shake than that, Mr Pessel.
Mr Pessel I wasn't — I could have done — I didn't know — really what was expected of me.
Mrs Bannion We must remember to do that next year. If you could note that down.
Ronnie I've already done so.
Mrs Bannion A good shake.
Wilf If you open the box now, we can allow the first ticket to be drawn. Keep seated please.
Ronnie Perhaps it would be right, here, to mention that anyone participating in this draw is debarred from holding a winning ticket.
Mrs Bannion We know that!
Ronnie Mr Pessel might not. Even though you bought tickets, Mr Pessel — they can't win.
Mr Pessel I didn't know that.
Mrs Bannion I knew it, but it didn't stop me buying ten books.
Ronnie We all bought tickets.

Mrs Bannion In the ten books I bought, I didn't even put my name on them. I buy to support the cause — building fund. I don't expect to win anything.
Mr Pessel And it wouldn't go down well with the other members if you did.
Mrs Bannion All blanks mine.
Wilf Will you draw out the first ticket, Mr Pessel. This is drawing for the first prize.
Mrs Bannion The food hamper.

Mr Pessel makes great play of drawing out the ticket which he then holds up

Wilf Hand it to me please.

Wilf unfolds the ticket

First prize of food hamper and whisky goes to ... (*reading*) "Mr P. Booker, 21 Chesswell Drive, Stanmount."

Pause

Ronnie Booker!
Wilf Stanmount!
Ronnie It's gone to a good address anyway.
Mrs Bannion You know who it is, don't you? Booker's Garages ... Booker's Garages ...? Down at the roundabout there?
Mr Pessel I know.
Mrs Bannion Booker's Sales and Services. He's got three garages in this town.
Mr Pessel Booker's Car Hire — that's it...
Mrs Bannion His father was a night watchman, did you know that?
Mr Pessel I didn't but I heard he'd improved himself.
Mrs Bannion Got a young wife, too.
Mr Pessel Goes with the job, eh.
Mrs Bannion My son represents a battery firm — round regular to Booker's.

Mr Pessel He's a big man in this town — and I picked his ticket — there you are.
Mrs Bannion What I'm worrying about now, is some of the food in that hamper. If I'd known it was going to somebody like that ...
Mr Pessel Well ...
Mrs Bannion I wouldn't have gone so much for the tins of stew. Something more to — nibble at.
Ronnie You can't go changing it now, Mrs Bannion.
Mrs Bannion I'm not changing — rearranging.
Ronnie I think the hamper should stay as seen.
Mrs Bannion It's not you that's responsible for choice. It's my name that goes on the card.
Ronnie What card?
Mrs Bannion The little card I put with the food. Selected by Mrs Bannion.
Ronnie I never knew we did that!
Mrs Bannion Always done it. Had people congratulate me.
Mr Pessel When you think of it — 1 could have picked any of these tickets. But I picked his.

Wilf stands up

Wilf (*with importance*) While we're all congratulating ourselves on whose ticket we picked, I'd like to remind you of what sort of club we're running here — and the purpose of this raffle. This is a social club for people like ourselves, who after a day's work, like to relax over a drink or play a game of cards or snooker. The proceeds of this raffle go to maintaining the fabric of the building which houses these activities. We all of us here bought tickets knowing that we couldn't win, because we have a commitment and interest in seeing that the club continues. I'm sure a lot of the members gave in the same spirit. I know for a fact that many of them, had they won the prize, were ready to hand it back to be given to someone more in need than themselves. They see the raffle as an opportunity to contribute to club funds, not as a chance to win a prize. They would say, and rightly in my opinion, that the prize should go to them who would otherwise be going without this Christmas. In this club we've always promoted a concern for welfare. You know yourselves some of the things we've done for the old folk. And more important what we hope to do in the future when we get started on the extension — because to be quite honest until we get that extra room that allows us to extend our facilities to provide special evenings for the old folks, I don't think we can call ourselves social. Bearing that in mind, I just think it's a bit unfortunate that the first prize should go to someone who neither needs it nor deserves it.

Pause

I thought that should be said.
Mr Pessel It's the old saying, money goes to money.
Wilf If it's an old saying, Mr Pessel, don't you think it's time we buried it?
Mr Pessel Oh — yes.
Mrs Bannion But you see, Wilf, a man like Booker, he might have bought twenty books of tickets.
Wilf I don't believe that for a minute. He's no interest in the club. He's not a member. He's never been inside the door.
Mrs Bannion We were glad to take his money for the ticket.
Wilf I don't mind him buying a ticket, I object to him winning the prize. The likes of him should be sold a special ticket — a sort of non-voting ticket — one that automatically disqualifies him from winning the prize. Is there anything that would allow us to do that in the future, Ronnie?
Ronnie It's never been done before, not to my recollection.
Mrs Bannion It wouldn't work, Wilf. Only those with a direct interest in helping the club would buy a ticket. You wouldn't have sold one to Mr Booker.
Wilf That says a lot about the man. He only bought a ticket because he wanted to win the food hamper — and that's a man with millions.
Ronnie It would need to be printed on the ticket, as a condition of sale.
Wilf Who sold him the ticket anyway?

Mrs Bannion My son. Sold to all of his clients — did very well for this club.

Wilf When you think of all those pensioners, clutching their one ticket, hoping this Christmas there'll be food on the table.

Ronnie Yes — in a way, it's a pity we shook the box.

Wilf That's what I'm coming to think. Always better to leave things as they are. That's why I was against shaking it.

Mr Pessel I wasn't bothered about shaking it either. If you had said leave it ...

Ronnie It was your decision to shake it.

Mr Pessel Only a little shake.

Wilf But the right shake for Mr Booker. Any other kind of shake would have been for somebody else.

Mrs Bannion You're not blaming Mr Pessel for the way things have turned out.

Wilf Of course I'm not blaming Mr Pessel!

Mr Pessel Chance, that's all it is.

Wilf Is that all it is, Mr Pessel, chance? We don't have any beliefs, we don't have a commitment for change, we just leave it to chance?

Mr Pessel I don't think I'm saying that.

Wilf We're all victims of our fate — everything we've worked towards in this club, it doesn't count — it turns out how it turns out anyway?

Mr Pessel Well no, I mean, there's social chance isn't there — I mean change.

Wilf I've sat on plenty committees in my time. Mrs Bannion there will vouch for it. She's heard me speak out against injustice, and never mind the world, I'm talking right here in our doorstep.

Mrs Bannion I don't think there's anyone done more than myself.

Wilf Of course, Mrs Bannion. And we've seen the results.

Mrs Bannion The big TV in the old folks. I got that installed.

Wilf That wasn't chance.

Mrs Bannion Chance had nothing to do with it.

Wilf Mr Pessel here is asking us to believe in chance.

Mr Pessel Oh that was only to do with the raffle ticket. I was only talking about drawing the raffle.

Wilf Well of course that was chance.

Mr Pessel That's all I was saying.

Wilf But it's not chance we take this food hamper up the tree-lined avenues of Stanmount and not down the streets of Craigton. That's our decision. Can you see the situation we're being forced into? Into taking a step that we don't want to take; to giving someone something that he doesn't need. He knows he doesn't need it; we know he doesn't need it, and yet, there's nothing we can do about it. Why? Because we're prepared to be bound by a game of chance. The luck of the draw. As if we were too stupid to make our own decision.

Pause

Mr Pessel Isn't it because it's the only fair way to do it?

Wilf For God's sake, can't you see it's the exact opposite of fair?

Ronnie It's unfortunate. It's unfortunate that was the ticket Mr Pessel drew out. If only he had picked another one.

Mr Pessel I should have stuck to the first ticket I touched. I had hold of another one but I let it go and went to this one.

Pause

Wilf You had hold of another ticket first?

Mr Pessel Only briefly you understand.

Pause

Wilf It's a false draw then. It's a false draw!

Mr Pessel Not having done it before ...

Wilf You're not being blamed, Mr Pessel. But I don't see how we can allow the draw to stand.

Mrs Bannion No, as long as he didn't change the ticket after he brought it out the box.

Wilf Our responsibility doesn't just start outside the box. We've a right to be concerned what happens inside the box! What do you think, Ronnie?

Luck of the Draw 13

Ronnie It's a new one on me, Wilf. I can't think there's anything in the rules about it.
Mrs Bannion As long as you bring only one ticket from the box, the draw is correct.
Ronnie Are you quoting from a rule book there?
Mrs Bannion It's how I've always seen it.
Ronnie We'd want more official direction than that.
Wilf Mr Pessel there had the courage to admit his mix-up inside the box. He could have kept quiet but he spoke out. I don't think we can ignore the man's admission.
Ronnie It certainly has to be considered.
Mrs Bannion Well I've considered it and I don't see how any other ticket in that box has a better claim to the prize than the one that was picked.
Ronnie We have to consider all the tickets. It's not right to make a special case for one.
Mrs Bannion I'm not making a special case.
Mr Pessel When you asked me here tonight, I never thought it would be this difficult.
Ronnie We have a duty to every one of those tickets in that box, Mr Pessel.
Mr Pessel I'm very impressed with the way you're treating them. I'm only sorry for my part that I fluffed it.
Wilf All credit to you for admitting it.
Mr Pessel I've admitted it, and I stand by it.
Wilf Then I don't see how we can call ourselves a fair committee if we were to ignore you. What's the legal position here, Ronnie?
Ronnie Well as I said, it's without precedent — but going on Mr Pessel's admission ...
Wilf I'd like to put forward we ask Mr Pessel to draw again for first prize.
Ronnie I think I'd have to second that ...
Mrs Bannion I don't know. I don't know about this at all.
Wilf I understand you hesitating, Mrs Bannion. But I know how delighted you would be if some deserving case won the prize. This way we're giving them another chance. I don't think you would want to deny them that.

Mrs Bannion I've no particular desire for Booker to get it.
Wilf But he will if we don't draw again.

Pause

I suggest we put it to the man who is here to judge fair practice. Mr Pessel, do you think the draw should stand, or do you think the fairest answer would be another draw?
Mr Pessel I think — another draw. As I see it this whole business has been carried on in the fairest possible way. It would be a great pity to let a draw stand if there was any doubt.
Wilf Well said, Mr Pessel
Mrs Bannion I'll go along with it. Why do you think I put the tins of stew in?
Ronnie That's drawing for the first prize — again.
Mrs Bannion First we put Mr Booker's ticket back in — that gives him another chance. I like to be fair.
Wilf This time give the box a good shake, Mr Pessel.

Mr Pessel shakes the box vigorously and then with great concentration draws out another ticket

Hand it to me, please. (*He opens the ticket*) Winner of the first prize is ... (*reading*) "Mrs A. Atkinson, Brook Cottage, Stanmount."

Pause

Ronnie Stanmount again.
Mrs Bannion Well if I'd known she was going to win it, I would never have allowed the draw to be taken again.
Ronnie You know her?
Mrs Bannion Brook Cottage, she's notorious. Starved her husband to death they say. Now she keeps all his money in a cupboard she can't shut the door on. Even the milk boy can't get his money out of her.
Ronnie Is that so?

Mrs Bannion I don't see how she could ever have bought a ticket, Wilf. This is what comes of making another draw. I knew I was against it.

Wilf I want to know who's been selling all these tickets up in Stanmount?

Mrs Bannion You did no service drawing out that one, Mr Pessel.

Wilf There must be tickets in there belonging to folks who deserve to win.

Ronnie It seems Mr Pessel has a touch for the rich ones.

Mr Pessel I did it as fairly as I could.

Wilf Yet you managed to pick two from the best area in town.

Mr Pessel Isn't it chance?

Mrs Bannion It's not chance ... I'll tell you what it is. The price of the tickets is too high. That's what it is.

Wilf You were on the committee when we voted on these prices, Mrs Bannion.

Mrs Bannion I went along with it, but I said to the others at the time ... Didn't I say it to you, Ronnie?

Ronnie I don't remember that.

Mrs Bannion Course I did. I knew I was right when I couldn't sell to my regulars. They said they were too dear.

Ronnie I have to admit I had something of the same reception myself.

Mrs Bannion I knew I had said it to you.

Wilf But we had to ask that price or we wouldn't have reached our target. And it was justified because we sold every ticket.

Mrs Bannion You see who you sold them to. Only the better off could afford them — that's why their tickets are coming up now.

Wilf You're not telling me that all those tickets in there belong to the well-off. I've got my regulars buy tickets off me every year — never mind what the price is.

Mrs Bannion So have I.

Wilf Well why aren't we picking them — they're in the box?

Mr Pessel You probably won't agree with this, Mr Chairman, but don't you have to put a certain amount down to luck?

Wilf Luck! You're right, Mr Pessel. This is typical of the luck these people have. In my experience you're more likely to sell a ticket to a poor widow than you are to one of them — and yet — these two get drawn first. That's proof if anything that, there's no fairness in luck.

Pause

Mrs Bannion I wouldn't want to see her winning it.
Wilf Nor I. As a social club we should be using this opportunity at this time of year to spread a little goodwill in the neighbourhood. Surely that's not beyond us?
Mrs Bannion I'd rather throw it away than see that one get it.
Wilf You and I could name half a dozen people whose life would be brighter if they were to win that hamper.
Mrs Bannion There's a dozen at least I could take it round.
Wilf Christmas. Isn't that what the spirit is all about?
Mrs Bannion I had them in mind when I bought the tins of stew.
Wilf You probably know a few old people, Mr Pessel, I know Ronnie does.
Mr Pessel Yeah, I keep meaning to visit them but …
Wilf Scraps for their Christmas dinner.
Mr Pessel It's tragic.
Wilf Tragic. And what is tragic — a lot of their tickets are in that box right now.
Ronnie Just waiting to be picked — pity you didn't, Mr Pessel.
Mr Pessel I feel bad about that.
Mrs Bannion It would have been nice to see one of the old ones getting it.
Ronnie That ticket you touched and didn't draw out in the first draw — that could have been someone in great need. Who knows.
Mrs Bannion That's what I was thinking.
Ronnie Pity.
Mr Pessel Yeh.

Pause

Wilf Can we really be happy about any of the draw now, bearing in mind the way Mr Pessel mixed up the first one? What do you think, Ronnie?

Luck of the Draw 17

Ronnie Yes, we want to be fair to the ticket that wasn't picked.
Mrs Bannion We have to be.
Wilf What worries me now is that Mr Pessel may think — this is carrying fairness to extremes ... That we're showing too much concern for correctness.
Mr Pessel Oh no, I would never go against a proper code of practice.
Wilf I want this to be a fair draw, Mr Pessel. I feel strongly about that. So strongly, I know I could put my own hand in that box and draw out the ticket of someone deserving to win.
Mr Pessel I think you probably could.
Wilf Of course, on one level, you could say that was irregular. You were brought here to make the draw, Mr Pessel. It's not for me to ...

Mr Pessel stands

Mr Pessel But what's regular, Mr Chairman? What's chance when you haven't got a chance? I know I've let you down tonight by the tickets I've picked — but it could be that this is an unlucky night for me. Everything I'm doing is acting against what I want to do. It's possible, isn't it? The more draws I make, the more unfair it's becoming. I never thought of it like this, but I could be working against chance. As if, I'm not giving chance, a chance.

Pause

Wilf That's very well put, Mr Pessel.
Mr Pessel I've said it and I'll stand by it. (*He sits*)
Mrs Bannion Make the draw, Wilf — you couldn't do any worse.
Wilf I'm prepared to, if there are no objections.
Ronnie But you understand, Mr Pessel, this is not normal practice. It's only being taken because — well it would have to be kept between those present tonight. Those who haven't seen how the situation evolved — they may not understand.
Mr Pessel I understand absolutely.
Mrs Bannion Make the draw, Wilf.

Wilf I won't shake it this time. (*He picks a ticket and opens it, reading*) "H. Hegly, 12 Glentally Road, Beathall"
Ronnie Beathall?
Mrs Bannion The new private estate.
Ronnie Young executives and book representatives.
Mrs Bannion Council tenants once removed.
Ronnie But a good area. A Christmas tree in every window.
Wilf I was sure I was going to do better than that.
Ronnie Certainly they'll be heavily into debt, but you couldn't say deserving. Not in the traditional way.

Pause

Wilf You want to have a go, Ronnie?
Ronnie I could.
Wilf Go to the bottom of the pile — that's where you'll find the poor.

Ronnie makes great play of rummaging through the tickets in the box without looking and then draws a ticket

Wilf Just the address.
Ronnie London!
Wilf London? We're not sending it there.
Mrs Bannion I'll pick a good one for you.

Mrs Bannion has her own particular way of drawing a ticket

　E. Hunter.
Wilf Just the address.
Mrs Bannion Howes Chase.
Wilf For God's sake!
Ronnie Suburban residential. Private education.
Wilf Is there another box somewhere or what? None of us can find a poor person? I don't believe it!

Wilf digs his hand in the box followed by the others. They open tickets searching for a really poor area of town until Mr Pessel turns up something unusual

Luck of the Draw

Mr Pessel This one's blank!

The rest stop picking

   Blank! Look!
Mrs Bannion Blank, that's mine! I put in the blank ones!
Mr Pessel Nothing on it.
Mrs Bannion That's right, it's mine! Remember, I told you!
Ronnie You can't claim on it.
Mrs Bannion Of course I'm not claiming on it. I'm just saying it was me that put them in blank. You don't think I would have put them in blank if I wanted to claim on it? Don't be stupid!
Ronnie You said it was yours.
Mrs Bannion It is mine.
Ronnie You don't know that. Others may have put them in blank.
Mrs Bannion What?
Ronnie With the same good intentions.
Mrs Bannion There's nothing on that ticket is there, Mr Pessel?
Mr Pessel Nothing.
Mrs Bannion Exactly! So there.
Wilf If I could remind you why we're here tonight — to pick a winner. All we've been getting so far is the rise of the middle-class. Which proves to me this whole pot luck system is weighted against us. It seems to me we've got the solution here in our own hands. I wonder if any of you can see it?

Pause

Ronnie We still have to be guided by the rules, Wilf.
Wilf All above board. I wouldn't have it any other way. We've picked the winning ticket. Can't you see it?
Mrs Bannion Could be any of them.
Wilf It's the blank one!
Ronnie That's nobody's ticket.
Mrs Bannion It's mine but I'm not claiming on it.
Wilf Three doors down from me there's an old pensioner, in his eighties — came out of hospital two weeks ago — major

operation. A man who worked all his days — now on his own — hardly sees a person from one day to the next. I'd like to write his name on that ticket.

Pause

Ronnie Yes.

Mr Pessel It's a good thought.

Ronnie It's the ideal winner. It's the one we were hoping Mr Pessel would pick.

Wilf And he did — once I put the old fellow's name on it.

Mr Pessel I'm certainly proud to have picked it.

Ronnie It's an interpretation of a regulation but not out with the rules.

Wilf I can put his name down?

Ronnie Yes.

Mr Pessel I second that.

Mrs Bannion Except — I can't help thinking of an old couple — used to live two blocks away from me. That is until they got them out. Stuck them up in one of those sky towers. Lived all their lives in the one home — now they're up in the clouds. She can't walk and he's frightened to look out the window. Be nice to take them round a surprise.

Pause

Wilf This old boy I'm talking about — while he was in hospital — place broken into, couldn't find anything worth taking, so they put the boot through his telly. That was his only company.

Mrs Bannion Course it's left to the old man to do the shopping. He can be away a day trying to find his way back up.

Wilf The old boy could make a food hamper like that last him a month.

Mrs Bannion The thing about the couple: it would be two getting the benefit.

Wilf Fair enough but it was my idea.

Mrs Bannion It's my ticket.

Luck of the Draw 21

Ronnie You said you weren't claiming on it.
Mrs Bannion Not for me, for the old couple!
Ronnie Wilf has a deserving case too.
Mr Pessel If only we could give them both a hamper.
Wilf It's a kind thought, Mr Pessel, but if we did that to all the deserving, we wouldn't make any money from the raffle. Remember the money we get from the raffle will be for their benefit. It all adds to the money we need for the extension. Once we get that extra room next year, we'll have old folks' nights once a week. It'll be cheap beer and ramps for wheelchairs — then we call ourselves a social club.
Ronnie I don't think it'll be next year, Wilf — not if you're relying on bar profits and raffles. I have the figures. I was keeping them for the AGM, but I can tell you now — it won't be next year.
Wilf Surely?
Ronnie No. Truth is as a club, we're no longer able to support ourselves.
Wilf Not able to support ourselves?
Ronnie I'm already composing a letter to the bank.
Wilf Why didn't I know this?
Ronnie I was frightened to tell you.
Mrs Bannion We're here to draw a raffle!
Ronnie Of course.
Mrs Bannion On the subject, I've got a suggestion to make. It's controversial and you'll probably shout me down but I'm going to make it anyway. We award the first prize to the first ticket picked.
Wilf You can't do that!
Ronnie No.
Wilf Not if you want to call it fair.
Mrs Bannion I think you can.
Wilf What about your old couple — the deserving cases?
Mrs Bannion Maybe I'm thinking about them more than anybody else. I'm looking ahead. Mr Booker wins the prize. Mr Booker is an important man in this town, a man of influence.
Ronnie That's true.

Mrs Bannion For him to win the food hamper. Nothing to him but he might never have won a raffle in his life. He's not going to forget the club that presented it to him. We make the gesture, it could bring reward, when we're looking for assistance with the extension.
Wilf Yes, but ...
Ronnie We won't do it on our own.
Mrs Bannion If we could get Booker behind us.
Ronnie It all comes down to cash, Wilf.
Wilf But we don't want to start corrupting ourselves for the sake of advantage. We still have to stand by personally what we decide.
Mrs Bannion He did win the draw.
Wilf Certainly that's in his favour.
Ronnie Before we came into this room tonight we had all decided we would stand by the draw. Whichever ticket came out first, that would be the winner. That's what we've done.
Mrs Bannion It could be the best winning ticket we've ever had.
Wilf But are we being fair?
Mr Pessel Very fair.
Wilf If that's the view of all here ...
Mr Pessel Something made me pick it. My hand was drawn to it. That's the attraction of the self made man.
Ronnie Chance never comes by chance.
Wilf At least it stops us discriminating between the old folks.

Mrs Bannion goes to the hamper and starts rearranging

Mrs Bannion Changes'll need to be made here. Upgrading. Delicatessen items and wine will have to be substituted for this. This is going to a man of discrimination. I won't trust anybody else to deliver it. I'll be taking it myself.
Ronnie I'd like to go with you, in case he has any financial queries about the club.
Wilf Are you quite satisfied with the fairness of the proceedings so far, Mr Pessel?
Mr Pessel More than satisfied. The work you've all put in tonight — it's been out of all proportion to fairness.

Luck of the Draw 23

Mrs Bannion returns from the hamper

Mrs Bannion I'll be presenting a shopping list for additional delicacies. This has to be seen as an investment.
Ronnie They say he has an indoor pool tip there at Stanmount.
Mrs Bannion And with en suite hospitality bar.
Wilf We should present ourselves as a small delegation. All the more to help carry the hamper, the size it's going to be. We'll get dressed up and hope to make a night of it.
Mrs Bannion 'Cause we're bringing him good news.
Ronnie Maybe good news in a bad day.
Wilf The only thing that worries me — is this winning ticket on the notice-board. I know what the members are going to say — rich man winning — that's how it is in life — the poor get nothing — it's all loaded against them ... They'll accuse me of fixing the result. What do I say to that?
Mr Pessel That's nothing to do with you. Luck of the draw, that's what you say, luck of the draw.

Black-out

THE END

FURNITURE AND PROPERTY LIST

On stage: Long table. *On it*: sheet of paper and pen
              Four hard chairs
              Table. *On it*: raffle prizes. 1st prize: large food hamper with some tins of stew, bottle of whisky, bottle of sherry. Other prizes: boxes of chocolates and bottles

Off stage: Large tin-box with a padlock containing raffle tickets (**Ronnie**)

Personal: **Mr Pessel**: door key
              Ronnie: brown envelope containing padlock key

LIGHTING PLOT

Practical fittings required: nil
1 interior. The same scene throughout

To open: General interior lighting

Cue 1   **Mr Pessel**: "… what you say, luck of the draw."   (Page 23)
Black-out

EFFECTS PLOT

No cues

www.ingramcontent.com/pod-product-compliance
Lightning Source LLC
Chambersburg PA
CBHW070455050426
42450CB00012B/3287